Reco⟩
S h a m e

Dale & Juanita Ryan

6 Studies for
Groups or Individuals

With Notes for Leaders

■ *L I F E R E C O V E R Y G U I D E S*

INTERVARSITY PRESS
DOWNERS GROVE, ILLINOIS 60515

InterVarsity Press is the book-publishing division of InterVarsity Christian Fellowship, a student movement active on campus at hundreds of universities, colleges and schools of nursing in the United States of America, and a member movement of the International Fellowship of Evangelical Students. For information about local and regional activities, write Public Relations Dept., InterVarsity Christian Fellowship, 6400 Schroeder Rd., P.O. Box 7895, Madison, WI 53707-7895.

Distributed in Canada through InterVarsity Press, 860 Denison St., Unit 3, Markham, Ontario L3R 4H1, Canada.

All Scripture quotations, unless otherwise indicated, are from the Holy Bible, New International Version. Copyright © 1973, 1978, International Bible Society. Used by permission of Zondervan Bible Publishers.

Cover illustration: Tim Nyberg

ISBN 0-8308-1153-2

Printed in the United States of America

12	11	10	9	8	7	6	5	4	3	2	1
99	98	97	96	95	94	93	92	91	90		

An Invitation to Recovery

Life Recovery Guides are rooted in four basic convictions.

First, we are in need of recovery. The word *recovery* implies that something has gone wrong. Things are not as they should be. We have sinned. We have been sinned against. We are entangled, stuck, bogged down, bound and broken. We need to be healed.

Second, recovery is a commitment to change. Because of this, recovery is a demanding process and often a lengthy one. There are no quick fixes in recovery. It means facing the truth about ourselves, even when that truth is painful. It means giving up our old destructive patterns and learning new life-giving patterns. Recovery means taking responsibility for our lives. It is not easy. It is sometimes painful. And it will take time.

Third, recovery is possible. No matter how hopeless it may seem, no matter how deeply we have been wounded by life or how often we have failed, recovery is possible. Our primary basis for hope in the process of recovery is that God is able to do things which we cannot do ourselves. Recovery is possible because God has committed himself to us.

Finally, these studies are rooted in the conviction that the Bible can be a significant resource for recovery. Many people who have lived through difficult life experiences have had bits of the Bible thrown at their pain as a quick fix or a simplistic solution. As a result, many people expect the Bible to be a barrier to recovery rather than a resource. These studies are based on the belief that the Bible is not a book of quick fixes and simplistic solutions. It is, on the contrary, a practical and helpful resource for recovery.

We were deeply moved personally by these biblical texts as we worked on this series. We are convinced that the God of the Bible can bring serenity to people whose lives have become unmanageable. If you are looking for resources to help you in your recovery, we invite you to study the Bible with an open mind and heart.

Getting the Most from Life Recovery Guides

Life Recovery Guides are designed to assist you to find out for yourself what the Bible has to say about different aspects of recovery. The texts you will study will be thought-provoking, challenging, inspiring and very personal. It will become obvious that these studies are not designed merely to convince you of the truthfulness of some idea. Rather, they are designed to allow biblical truths to renew your heart and mind.

We want to encourage realistic expectations of these discussion guides. First, they are not intended to be everything-the-Bible-says about any subject. They are not intended to be a systematic presentation of biblical theology.

Second, we want to emphasize that these guides are not intended to provide a recovery program or to be a substitute for professional counseling. If you are in a counseling relationship or are involved in a support group, we pray that these studies will enrich that resource. If you are not in a counseling relationship and your recovery involves long-term issues, we encourage you to consider seeking the assistance of a mental health professional.

What these guides are designed to do is to help you study a series of biblical texts which relate to the process of recovery. Our hope is that they will allow you to discover the Good News for people who are struggling to recover.

There are six studies in each Life Recovery Guide. This should provide you with maximum flexibility in how you use these guides. Combining the guides in various ways will allow you to adapt them to your time schedule and to focus on the concerns most important to you or your group.

All of the studies in this series use a workbook format. Space is provided for writing answers to each question. This is ideal for personal study and allows group members to prepare in advance for the discussion. The guides also contain leader's notes with suggestions on how to lead a group discussion. The notes provide additional background information on certain questions, give helpful tips on group dynamics and suggest ways to deal with problems that may arise during the discussion. These features enable someone with little or no experience to lead an effective discussion.

Suggestions for Individual Study

1. As you begin each study, pray that God would bring healing and recovery to you through his Word.

2. After spending time in personal reflection, read and reread the passage to be studied.

3. Write your answers in the spaces provided or in a personal journal. Writing can bring clarity and deeper understanding of yourself and of the Bible. For the same reason, we suggest that you write out your prayers at the end of each study.

4. Use the leader's notes at the back of the guide to gain additional insight and information.

5. Share what you are learning with someone you trust. Recovery is empowered by experiences of community.

Suggestions for Group Study

Even if you have already done these studies individually, we strongly encourage you to find some way to do them with a group of other people as well. Although each person's recovery is different, everyone's recovery is empowered by the mutual support and encouragement that can only be found in a one-on-one or a group setting. Several reminders may be helpful for participants in a group study:

1. Realize that trust grows over time. If opening up in a group setting is risky, realize that you do not have to share more than what feels safe to you. However, taking risks is a necessary part of recovery. So, do participate in the discussion as much as you are able.

2. Be sensitive to the other members of the group. Listen attentively when they talk. You will learn from their insights. If you can, link what you say to the comments of others so the group stays on the topic. Also, be affirming whenever you can. This will encourage some of the more hesitant members of the group to participate.

3. Be careful not to dominate the discussion. We are sometimes so eager to share what we have learned that we do not leave opportunity for others to respond. By all means participate! But allow others to do so as well.

4. Expect God to teach you through the passage being discussed and through the other members of the group. Pray that you will have a profitable time together.

5. We recommend that groups follow a few basic guidelines, and that these guidelines be read at the beginning of each discussion session. The guidelines, which you may wish to adapt to your situation, are:

a. Anything said in the group is considered confidential and will not be discussed outside the group unless specific permission is given to do so.

b. We will provide time for each person present to talk if he or she feels comfortable doing so.

c. We will talk about ourselves and our own situations, avoiding conversation about other people.

d. We will listen attentively to each other.

e. We will be very cautious about giving advice.

f. We will pray for each other.

If you are the discussion leader, you will find additional suggestions and helpful ideas for each study in the leader's notes. These are found at the back of the guide.

Recovering from Shame

Shame is a common social experience. It is rooted in exchanges between people. It may grow out of experiences of public humiliation. It may result from experiences of being devalued. It may come from experiences of rejection.

Many people learn shame early in life in their families-of-origin. Harsh criticism, neglect, lack of affirmation, humiliation, contempt and ridicule are not uncommon features of family life. Any of these experiences can contribute to shame in family members.

The family is not, however, the only source of shaming experiences. Shame learned in families is often reinforced by other relationships and in other systems, such as school and work settings. And shame is sometimes fostered by experiences in the Christian community. Experiences of public exposure, judgment and rejection sometimes happen in the name of Christ.

Whatever the source, shame is a very painful emotional experience. Shame hurts at a fundamental level.

While shame is rooted in social experiences, it is also easily internalized. If people experience humiliation often enough, intensely enough, or consistently enough, they may come to the conclusion that they ought to be humiliated. When shame becomes internalized in this way, it poses a fundamental threat to a person's identity.

There is an important difference between guilt and shame. Guilt is part of recognizing that we have done something wrong. Guilt is a painful emotion. It can, however, be a helpful emotion because it alerts us to a violation of our values and ideals. Guilt can be the first step in a process which leads to growth and change, to repentance and recovery. Shame, on the other hand, is not part of such a healthy process. Shame does not open a person to the possibility of change. Instead, shame is experienced as a flaw so fundamental that no hope for recovery seems possible. Shame causes people to see themselves as unlovable, unworthy and irreparable.

Perhaps the most difficult tenet of the Christian gospel to believe is that no matter how badly damaged you think you are, God sees you as valuable. No matter how unlovable you may seem to yourself, God loves you. No matter how pessimistic about the possibility of recovering from shame you may be, God is eager to bring healing.

Because shame damages a person so deeply, recovery from shame will require deep healing. This kind of healing requires time and the help of others who love you. Because recovery from shame is such a difficult journey, it is vitally important to know that God is prepared to be helpful. The Bible is full of stories about shame and about God's response to shame. The studies which follow are designed to help you decide for yourself about God's response to people who have experienced shame.

Will God reinforce your experiences of shame? Will he humiliate you? Does he devalue you? Does he hold you in contempt? Does he agree with your self-contempt?

In preparing these studies we were deeply moved by the clarity of Scripture about God's unconditional love for us. We encourage you to approach these texts with an openness to hear God's Word to you. Our prayer is that you will hear the voice of God clearly calling you by name, speaking tenderly, eager to heal the scars left by experiences with shame.

May your roots sink deeply in the soil of God's love.

Dale and Juanita Ryan

1
The
Experience
of Shame

Jim raised his hand and asked for clarification of the professor's point.
It was the last time he would ever do that in class. The professor
responded with a ten-minute lecture which pointed out that the
question was stupid and the answer was obvious. It was an enter-
taining diatribe which had the rest of the class laughing. Jim felt
exposed, rejected and devalued. Jim experienced shame.

Shame, like anger or sorrow, is a painful emotion. Shame makes
a person want to disappear. "We stand revealed as lesser, painfully
diminished in our own eyes and the eyes of others as well."[1] Shame
is an isolating experience. We do not want to talk about our shame.
Shame makes us want to withdraw. If we cannot cover our shame
and hide, we put a good face on it. That is, we cover our shame with
pretending. We are ashamed of our shame.

The first step in recovery from shame is to acknowledge that it
is a part of our lives. The author of the text for this study cried out
to God in his time of shame. He moved out of hiding to describe both
the events which provoked the shame and the agony of his experience.

☐ Personal Reflection

1. Recall an experience which made you want to run and hide. Describe the experience briefly.

2. What feelings do you have as you remember this experience?

☐ Bible Study

In you, O LORD, I have taken refuge;
    let me never be put to shame;
    deliver me in your righteousness.
Turn your ear to me,
    come quickly to my rescue;
be my rock of refuge,
    a strong fortress to save me.
I hate those who cling to worthless idols;
    I trust in the LORD.

I will be glad and rejoice in your love,
    for you saw my affliction
    and knew the anguish of my soul.
You have not handed me over to the enemy

but have set my feet in a spacious place.

Be merciful to me, O LORD, for I am in distress;
    my eyes grow weak with sorrow,
    my soul and my body with grief.
My life is consumed by anguish
    and my years by groaning;
my strength fails because of my affliction,
    and my bones grow weak.
Because of all my enemies,
    I am the utter contempt of my neighbors;
I am a dread to my friends—
    those who see me on the street flee from me.
I am forgotten by them as though I were dead;
    I have become like broken pottery.
For I hear the slander of many;
    there is terror on every side;
they conspire against me
    and plot to take my life.

But I trust in you, O LORD;
    I say, "You are my God."
My times are in your hands;
    deliver me from my enemies
    and from those who pursue me.
Let your face shine on your servant;
    save me in your unfailing love. (Psalm 31:1-2, 6-16)

---

1. What insights did you gain during your time of personal reflection?

2. What kinds of experiences have contributed to the author's sense of shame?

3. How does the author describe the results of these experiences?

4. The author describes his experience by saying, "I have become like broken pottery." What does this picture suggest about the experience of shame?

5. How do the writer's experiences of shame compare with your own?

6. What does the writer ask from God?

7. What things lead him to express thanks to God?

8. At the beginning of the prayer, the author calls God "my rock of refuge, a strong fortress to save me." How would experiencing God as a rock and a refuge help you when you feel shame?

9. What could you do this week that would help you to feel less isolated and alone?

☐ **Prayer** _____

What would you like to share today with the God who is a rock and strong fortress?

---

[1]Gershen Kaufman, *Shame: The Power of Caring* (Cambridge, Mass.: Schenkman Publishing, 1985), p. 11.

2
The Shame
of Public
Exposure

*Three-year-old Joey was a pest during his ten-year-old sister's birth-*day party. In spite of his occasional attention-seeking distractions, people seemed to be having a good time. At one point, however, the fun and laughter abruptly halted as Joey's mother, by now tired and exasperated with Joey, grabbed him by the hand and took him into the family room. Addressing the room full of ten-year-old girls and the parents who were present, she said, "I can't believe it, but he just wet his pants again! He's still such a baby! It's terrible!" People laughed, and the party continued. No one seemed to notice that Joey had been publicly exposed and shamed.

Public exposure of our faults and weaknesses happens to all of us. We have all been laughed at. We have all had fingers pointed at us, or known others were talking about us behind our backs. We have all experienced the public exposure of our faults.

Often we simply accept experiences like this as part of life which, although undesirable, can be managed successfully without any significant damage to our identity. On other occasions, for a variety of reasons, such public exposure of our deficiencies produces shame. If the public exposure continues long enough or intensely enough, or if it is perpetuated by a parent or someone else who is significant to us, it can become more than a transitory emotion. Public humiliation can become part of our identity. We can come to see ourselves as fundamentally and irreparably deficient.

People who experience shame at these deep levels often conclude that they don't belong. They may find it difficult to feel like a meaningful participant in social groups. In addition they may find that the terror of being exposed interferes with the development of intimate relationships. Isolation and alienation may seem the only way to survive.

Clearly, one problem which shame creates for us is that we cannot grow as persons when we are running. We cannot be healed when we are hiding.

Jesus understood this. He knew the pain that can come from public exposure. He understood the fear of ridicule. He did not criticize people for being susceptible to shame. Rather, as we will see in this Bible study, his instincts were to say to people who had experienced shame: "You are the kind of person I am seeking. I want to spend time with you. You belong in my family."

□ **Personal Reflection** _____

1. Think of an experience of public exposure which resulted in your experiencing shame. Describe it briefly.

2. What impact did that experience have on you?

3. What words of acceptance do you need to hear as a result of that experience?

☐ **Bible Study** _____

Jesus entered Jericho and was passing through. A man was there by the name of Zacchaeus; he was a chief tax collector and was wealthy. He wanted to see who Jesus was, but being a short man he could not, because of the crowd. So he ran ahead and climbed a sycamore-fig tree to see him, since Jesus was coming that way.

When Jesus reached the spot, he looked up and said to him, "Zacchaeus, come down immediately. I must stay at your house today." So he came down at once and welcomed him gladly.

All the people saw this and began to mutter, "He has gone to be the guest of a 'sinner.' "

But Zacchaeus stood up and said to the Lord, "Look, Lord! Here and now I give half of my possessions to the poor, and if I have cheated anybody out of anything, I will pay back four times the amount."

Jesus said to him, "Today salvation has come to this house, be-

cause this man, too, is a son of Abraham. For the Son of Man came
to seek and to save what was lost." (Luke 19:1-9)

---

1. What insights did you gain from your time of personal reflection?

2. What do we know about Zacchaeus from the description in this
text?

3. In what ways might the crowd's response have contributed to
Zacchaeus's shame?

4. How does Jesus respond to Zacchaeus?

5. What changes in Zacchaeus appear to have been made possible by Jesus' public acceptance?

6. How do you think Zacchaeus felt when Jesus said, "This man, too, is a son of Abraham"?

7. Jesus states in clear and simple terms the purpose of his mission: "The Son of Man came to seek and save what was lost." This statement was a shocking reversal of expectations for people who believed God was interested only in "righteous" people. How is Jesus' mission good news for people who live in shame?

8. How does Jesus' response to Zacchaeus compare with how you expect God to respond to you?

9. Imagine that you are Zacchaeus. Listen to your crowd mutter. Notice the faces which appear in your crowd. Now notice Jesus. He approaches you. He calls you out. He directs the attention of the crowd to you and in front of them says to you: "I want to be with you. I have been looking for you. I came here to spend time with you. You belong. I love you." Meditate on this picture for a few minutes.

What were your thoughts and feelings during this meditation?

☐ **Prayer** ——————————————————————————————

What would you like to say today to the God who says, "You belong"?

3
The Shame
of Being
Devalued

People in families or groups which produce shame are often judged for their thoughts, feelings and actions. The standards used in these evaluations may have to do with how successful, how moral, how bright or how pious a person is. The standards may be arbitrary, may change unpredictably and may appeal to divine revelation for authority. The common thread in evaluations which lead to shame is the devaluing of the person who does not measure up. When people fall short of the standard, they are judged to be inadequate, damaged and undesirable. A lot is at risk in these evaluations because the worth of the person is being measured.

People in families and social groups which do not produce shame do not experience their worth being judged in this way. Mistakes and weaknesses are acknowledged and taken seriously, but the value of the person is not at risk. Problems, limitations, weaknesses and even moral evil are expected as part of our common human condition. In healthy families and groups these do not lead to judgment but are responded to with a combination of compassion, accountability and forgiveness. As a result, a person's sense of value remains intact.

Many religious systems, even some with orthodox theology, set up standards which are used to judge people's worth. If people do not meet these standards, they are devalued and shamed. Religiously reinforced shame was as common in Jesus' day as it is in our own. The religious leadership worked very hard to attain high personal moral standards. But they also devalued people whom they saw as "sinners." "Sinners" who did not meet the leader's standards were outcasts, untouchables, people of no value.

Jesus' response to "sinners" was a radical contrast to the shame-based religious systems of his time. Jesus did not devalue people because they did not meet a standard—no matter how godly the standard. Jesus valued sinners. Those people who appeared to others merely as moral failures Jesus saw as people of great worth.

☐ **Personal Reflection** _____

1. Think of a time when you felt devalued by someone who was important to you. What was the impact of that experience on you?

2. What words of valuing do you need to hear from God?

☐ Bible Study

Now one of the Pharisees invited Jesus to have dinner with him, so he went to the Pharisee's house and reclined at the table. When a woman who had lived a sinful life in that town learned that Jesus was eating at the Pharisee's house, she brought an alabaster jar of perfume, and as she stood behind him at his feet weeping, she began to wet his feet with her tears. Then she wiped them with her hair, kissed them and poured perfume on them.

When the Pharisee who had invited him saw this, he said to himself, "If this man were a prophet, he would know who is touching him and what kind of woman she is—that she is a sinner."

Jesus answered him, "Simon, I have something to tell you."

"Tell me, teacher," he said.

"Two men owed money to a certain moneylender. One owed him five hundred denarii, and the other fifty. Neither of them had the money to pay him back, so he canceled the debts of both. Now which of them will love him more?"

Simon replied, "I suppose the one who had the bigger debt canceled."

"You have judged correctly," Jesus said.

Then he turned toward the woman and said to Simon, "Do you see this woman? I came into your house. You did not give me any water for my feet, but she wet my feet with her tears and wiped them with her hair. You did not give me a kiss, but this woman, from the time I entered, has not stopped kissing my feet. You did not put oil on my head, but she has poured perfume on my feet. Therefore, I tell you, her many sins have been forgiven—for she loved much. But he who has been forgiven little loves little."

Then Jesus said to her, "Your sins are forgiven."

The other guests began to say among themselves, "Who is this who even forgives sins?"

Jesus said to the woman, "Your faith has saved you; go in peace." (Luke 7:36-50)

1. What insights did you gain during your time of personal reflection?

2. The text begins with Jesus accepting the devotion of a woman who had led "a sinful life in that town." How would you characterize the questions which this raised for Simon?

3. How might Simon's evaluation of the woman have contributed to her experience of shame?

4. Although Simon spoke "to himself," Jesus knew the shame-creating nature of Simon's attitude and responded with a story. What were the central concerns of the story Jesus told?

5. After telling the story, Jesus "turned toward the woman" but addresses Simon. The speech begins with a rhetorical question: "Do you see this woman?" What is the point of this question?

6. How does Jesus demonstrate his valuing of the woman?

7. How does Jesus' response to the woman compare with how you expect God to respond to you?

8. What experiences in the past have allowed you to see yourself as valued by God?

9. Imagine for a moment that you are the woman in this story. Listen to Jesus say to the Pharisees: "Look at this woman. She is a person, not an object or a category. She cannot be discounted, ignored or devalued. I love her. I am moved by her love for me."

Imagine Jesus saying these words about you. Reread these words, putting your name in place of the pronouns.

How might hearing this from Jesus help you to see yourself as valuable?

☐ **Prayer** _____

Respond to the God who values you.

4
The
Shame of
Rejection

Bill had always considered himself to be an introvert. He did not, for example, find it easy to stand up in front of groups. But, after he became a Christian during his freshman year in college, Bill found himself in leadership roles more and more. He was discovering that he was a gifted and capable leader with a deep compassion for others. Bill wanted to see his college group at church get involved in doing something meaningful for the homeless people who slept in the church basement on winter nights. Many in the group shared his concern and looked to Bill to lead the way.

Unfortunately Bill's involvement in leadership died a sudden death one day when he overheard three young men in the group talking about him. They were saying: "Who does he think he is anyway? I'm sick of Bill and all his ideas. He must really be on an ego trip. He's just trying to make a name for himself."

Rejection. It is one of the events which can trigger the painful emotion of shame. It can make us want to crawl back into a safe corner. We experience rejection when we are ignored, when we are left out, when we are inappropriately blamed, when we are misunderstood, or when our abilities are devalued.

Rejection is a common human experience. We have all encountered it at one time or another. It is important when we experience rejection to understand how God responds. When we feel like running and hiding, do we need to run and hide from God as well? Will he add to our shame? This study affirms that God does not reject us even when people do.

☐ **Personal Reflection** _____

1. Think of an experience you have had with rejection. Describe it briefly.

2. What was the impact of this experience on how you saw yourself?

3. What impact would it have had if this rejection had been justified by appeal to divine revelation?

☐ Bible Study

The apostles and the brothers throughout Judea heard that the Gentiles also had received the word of God. So when Peter went up to Jerusalem, the circumcised believers criticized him and said, "You went into the house of uncircumcised men and ate with them."

Peter began and explained everything to them precisely as it had happened: "I was in the city of Joppa praying, and in a trance I saw a vision. I saw something like a large sheet being let down from heaven by its four corners, and it came down to where I was. I looked into it and saw four-footed animals of the earth, wild beasts, reptiles, and birds of the air. Then I heard a voice telling me, 'Get up, Peter. Kill and eat.'

"I replied, 'Surely not, Lord! Nothing impure or unclean has ever entered my mouth.'

"The voice spoke from heaven a second time, 'Do not call anything impure that God has made clean.' This happened three times, and then it was all pulled up to heaven again.

"Right then three men who had been sent to me from Caesarea stopped at the house where I was staying. The Spirit told me to have no hesitation about going with them. These six brothers also went with me, and we entered the man's house. He told us how he had seen an angel appear in his house and say, 'Send to Joppa for Simon who is called Peter. He will bring you a message through which you and all your household will be saved.'

"As I began to speak, the Holy Spirit came on them as he had come on us at the beginning. Then I remembered what the Lord had said: 'John baptized with water, but you will be baptized with the Holy Spirit.' So if God gave the same gift as he gave us, who believed in the Lord Jesus Christ, who was I to think that I could oppose God?"

When they heard this, they had no further objections and praised God, saying, "So then, God has granted even the Gentiles repentance unto life" (Acts 11:1-18).

1. What insights did you gain during your time of personal reflection?

2. The home Peter visited was that of Cornelius. Because Cornelius and his friends were uncircumcised (that is, not practicing Jews), Peter was hesitant to visit them, and later was criticized for eating in Cornelius's home. What impact might the kind of rejection Cornelius experienced have?

3. The rejection of Cornelius was rooted in religious convictions. In what ways is this kind of religious justification of rejection especially painful and shaming?

4. What did God do to make his acceptance of Cornelius clear?

5. Peter's behavior and attitudes changed toward Cornelius after he realized that God accepted Cornelius. What impact do you think Peter's visit had on Cornelius?

6. In addition to Peter's acceptance, the church leadership in Jerusalem came to accept what God had done. How might this acceptance by the church leadership make it easier for Cornelius and members of his household to recover from their experience of rejection?

7. How could it help you in your struggle with shame to know that God does not reject you?

8. Peter demonstrated his acceptance of Cornelius by visiting him and by sharing a meal. What practical things can you do to demonstrate your acceptance of others?

9. What practical demonstrations of acceptance by others would help you in your recovery?

☐ **Prayer** _____

What do you want to tell the One who accepts you?

5
Internalized
Shame

Being publicly exposed, being devalued and being rejected are all experiences which can produce the painful emotion of shame. Shame, like fear, anger or sadness, is an emotion which everyone has experienced. For many people, however, experiences of this kind are so acute or so frequent that shame begins to become more than a passing painful emotion. Over time shame can work its way into the core of a person's identity. It can become central to how people perceive themselves.

Once shame has become internalized, people can experience shame in response to their internal promptings. It is not necessary for another person to expose, devalue or reject them. In this way the painful experience of shame becomes a daily reality.

Due in part to a failure to distinguish between guilt and shame, many Christians have mistakenly taken the experience of shame to be a necessary starting point for spiritual growth. As a consequence, many Christians find it difficult to feel good about their relationship with God unless they feel badly about themselves. The low self-esteem that accompanies internalized shame, however, is not at all like true humility. Internalized shame is a kind of disabling self-hatred; it makes very poor soil for spiritual growth.

For Christians, recovery from shame requires that we learn to think and feel about ourselves in ways that are consistent with the way God thinks and feels about us.

The Scriptures show clearly that God does not expose us in ways that create shame. God does not see us as worthless. God does not reject us. God does not shame us. As we will see in this text, God welcomes those who live in shame, wraps his arms around them and throws a party in their honor.

□ **Personal Reflection** _____

1. The way we think and feel about ourselves has a profound effect on who we are. What kinds of negative messages (of rejection and devaluing) do you give to yourself?

2. What impact do these messages have on you?

3. What positive messages would contrast with these negative messages?

☐ Bible Study_____

"There was a man who had two sons. The younger one said to his father, 'Father, give me my share of the estate.' So he divided his property between them.

"Not long after that, the younger son got together all he had, set off for a distant country and there squandered his wealth in wild living. After he had spent everything, there was a severe famine in that whole country, and he began to be in need. So he went and hired himself out to a citizen of that country, who sent him to his fields to feed pigs. He longed to fill his stomach with the pods that the pigs were eating, but no one gave him anything.

"When he came to his senses, he said, 'How many of my father's hired men have food to spare, and here I am starving to death! I will set out and go back to my father and say to him: Father, I have sinned against heaven and against you. I am no longer worthy to be called your son; make me like one of your hired men.' So he got up and went to his father.

"But while he was still a long way off, his father saw him and was filled with compassion for him; he ran to his son, threw his arms around him and kissed him.

"The son said to him, 'Father, I have sinned against heaven and against you. I am no longer worthy to be called your son.'

"But the father said to his servants, 'Quick! Bring the best robe and put it on him. Put a ring on his finger and sandals on his feet. Bring the fattened calf and kill it. Let's have a feast and celebrate.

For this son of mine was dead and is alive again; he was lost and is found.' So they began to celebrate." (Luke 15:11-24)

---

1. What insights did you gain during your time of personal reflection?

2. In this story that Jesus told the younger son comes "to his senses" and realizes that his situation is desperate. What are the son's thoughts and feelings toward himself?

3. How might you feel about yourself if you were in this situation?

4. What does the son expect from his father?

5. What does the father do and say when the son returns?

6. How do the father's thoughts and feelings toward his son contrast with the son's thoughts and feelings about himself?

7. Clearly, Jesus intended the father in this story to be a picture of God our Father. How do the father's thoughts and feelings about the son compare to what you expect God to think and feel about you?

8. Like us, the son found it difficult to experience guilt without also experiencing shame. What might help you to experience appropriate guilt without being consumed by shame?

9. Imagine for a moment that you are the son in this parable. You are returning to God. You have experienced failure. You are practicing a speech to make which is full of internalized shame: "I am not worthy." "I don't deserve to belong to your family." But you see God running to greet you. He hugs you. He welcomes you. He is full of joy. Let yourself rest in God's arms. Feel his joy.

What thoughts and feelings do you have in response to this meditation?

☐ **Prayer** _____

Ask God to help you think and feel about yourself in ways that are consistent with his thoughts and feelings.

6
God's Love
for Those
in Shame

One of the most confusing aspects of shame is that we often feel shame about experiencing shame. Because shame is so uncomfortable and because we don't know what to do with this feeling, we tend to deny that it is part of our lives. Recovery from shame, however, requires that we acknowledge our shame so that we can begin to be free of its power.

The courage to acknowledge our shame comes from a growing awareness of God's love for us. Christian discipleship for people who have been trapped in shame is the process of learning that God does not contribute to our shame and does not want us to be bound by shame. He does not expose us; he provides a refuge for us. He does not devalue us; he declares us valuable. He does not reject us; he embraces us with arms of love.

It is not that God ignores our sins or our weakness. He does not pretend there is no problem. He takes our sin and weakness seriously. But he does not expose us or devalue us or reject us because of these things. With a full knowledge of who we are, God loves us.

In the text for this study the author, Paul, asserts that God loves us. As a consequence, no one can condemn us, not even our own internalized shame-voice. Nothing can keep God from loving us. Nothing will stop him from pursuing us in love. Nothing can separate us from his love. Nothing.

☐ Personal Reflection

1. What specific experiences might make it difficult for you to trust God when he says, "I am for you"?

2. Write a short prayer confessing how you tend to think and feel about yourself. Ask God to help you think and feel about yourself in ways that are consistent with his thoughts and feelings about you.

☐ Bible Study

If God is for us, who can be against us? He who did not spare his own Son, but gave him up for us all—how will he not also, along with him, graciously give us all things? Who will bring any charge against those whom God has chosen? It is God who justifies. Who is he that condemns? Christ Jesus, who died—more than that, who was raised to life—is at the right hand of God and is also interceding for us.

Who shall separate us from the love of Christ? Shall trouble or hardship or persecution or famine or nakedness or danger or sword? As it is written:
> "For your sake we face death all day long; we are considered as sheep to be slaughtered."

No, in all these things we are more than conquerors through him who loved us. For I am convinced that neither death nor life, neither angels nor demons, neither the present nor the future, nor any powers, neither height nor depth, nor anything else in all creation, will be able to separate us from the love of God that is in Christ Jesus our Lord. (Romans 8:31-39)

---

1. What insights did you gain during your time of personal reflection?

2. In the first part of this text Paul uses six rhetorical questions, which have the effect of emphasizing a truth. What truth is Paul emphasizing with these questions?

3. Paul provides a long list of things which seem to threaten God's love for us. One such potential threat comes from people who "bring a charge" against us or condemn us. How have experiences of condemnation seemed to threaten your relationship with God?

4. Paul includes troubles and hardships in the list of things which may seem to threaten God's love for us. During difficult times, we tend to think, "If I were a good Christian, this wouldn't be happening to me. Something must be wrong with me." How have troubles or hardships made you question your relationship with God?

5. In addition to condemnation and troubles, Paul lists a number of other experiences that might cause us to question God's love for us. What specific things in your life seem to threaten to separate you from God and his love?

6. What reasons does Paul give for feeling secure in God's love even though we experience condemnation, hardship and other perceived threats to our relationship?

7. How can Paul claim that "in all these things we are more than conquerors" when he has just said that life sometimes feels like facing death all day long?

8. How might resting securely in God's love help you in your struggle with the painful realities of life?

9. What could help you this week to remember that God is for you?

☐ **Prayer** _____

What do you want to express to the God who loves you?

Leader's Notes

You may be experiencing a variety of feelings as you anticipate leading a group using a Life Recovery Guide. You may feel inadequate and afraid of what will happen. If this is the case, know you are in good company. Many of the kings, prophets and apostles in the Bible felt inadequate and afraid. Many other small group leaders share the experience of fear as well.

Your willingness to lead, however, is a gift to the other group members. It might help if you tell them about your feelings and ask them to pray for you. Keep in mind that the other group members share the responsibility for the group. And realize that it is God's work to bring insight, comfort, healing and recovery to group members. Your role is simply to provide guidance for the discussion. The suggestions listed below will help you to provide that guidance.

Using the Life Recovery Guide Series
This Life Recovery Guide is one in a series of eight guides. The series was designed to be a flexible tool that can be used in various combinations by individuals and groups—such as support groups, Bible studies and Sunday-school classes. Each guide contains six studies. If all eight guides are used, they can provide a year-long curriculum series. Or if the guides are used in pairs, they can provide studies for a quarter (twelve weeks).

We want to emphasize that all of the guides in this series are designed to be useful to anyone. Each guide has a specific focus, but all are written with a general audience in mind. Additionally, the workbook format allows for personal interaction with biblical truths, making the guides adaptable to each individual's unique journey in recovery.

The four guides which all individuals and groups should find they can most easily relate to are *Recovery from Distorted Images of God, Recovery from Loss, Recovery from Bitterness* and *Recovery from Shame.* All of us need to replace our distorted images of God with biblically accurate images. All of us experience losses, disappointments and disillusionment in life, as well as loss through death or illness. We all have life experiences and relationships which lead to bitterness and which make forgiveness difficult. And we all experience shame and its debilitating consequences.

The four other guides are *Recovery from Codependency, Recovery from Family Dysfunctions, Recovery from Abuse* and *Recovery from Addictions.* Although these guides have a more specific focus, they address issues of very general concern both within the Christian community and in our culture as a whole. The biblical resources will be helpful to your recovery even if you do not share the specific concerns which these guides address.

Individuals who are working on a specific life issue and groups with a shared focus may want to begin with the guide which relates most directly to their concerns. Survivors of abuse, for example, may want to work through *Recovery from Abuse* and follow it with *Recovery from Shame.* Adult children from dysfunctional families may want to begin with *Recovery from Family Dysfunctions* and then use *Recovery from Distorted Images of God.* And those who struggle with addictive patterns may want to begin with *Recovery from Addictions* and then use *Recovery from Codependency.*

There are many other possibilities for study combinations. The short descriptions of each guide on the last page, as well as the information on the back of each guide will help you to further decide which guides will be most helpful to your recovery.

Preparing to Lead

1. Develop realistic expectations of yourself as a small group leader. Do not feel that you have to "have it all together." Rather, commit yourself to an ongoing discipline of honesty about your own needs. As you grow in honesty about your own needs, you will grow as well in your capacity for compassion, gentleness and patience with yourself and with others. As a leader, you can encourage an atmosphere of honesty by being honest about yourself.

2. Pray. Pray for yourself and your own recovery. Pray for the group members. Invite the Holy Spirit to be present as you prepare and as you meet.

3. Read the study several times.

4. Take your time to thoughtfully work through each question, writing out your answers.

5. After completing your personal study, read through the leader's notes for the study you are leading. These notes are designed to help you in several ways. First, they tell you the purpose the authors had in mind while writing the study. Take time to think through how the questions work together to accomplish that purpose. Second, the notes provide you with additional background information or comments on some of the questions. This information can be useful if people have difficulty understanding or answering a question. Third, the leader's notes can alert you to potential problems you may encounter during the study.

6. If you wish to remind yourself during the group discussion of anything mentioned in the leader's notes, make a note to yourself below that question in your study guide.

Leading the Study

1. Begin on time. You may want to open in prayer, or have a group member do so.

2. Be sure everyone has a study guide. Decide as a group if you want people to do the study on their own ahead of time. If your time together is limited, it will be helpful for people to prepare in advance.

3. At the beginning of your first time together, explain that these studies are meant to be discussions, not lectures. Encourage the members of the group to participate. However, do not put pressure on those who may be hesitant to speak during the first few sessions. Clearly state that people do not need to share anything they do not feel safe sharing. Remind people that it will take time to trust each other.

4. Read aloud the group guidelines listed in the front of the guide. These commitments are important in creating a safe place for people to talk and trust and feel.

5. The covers of the Life Recovery Guides are designed to incorporate both symbols of the past and hope for the future. During your first meeting, allow the group to describe what they see in the cover and respond to it.

6. Read aloud the introductory paragraphs at the beginning of the discussion for the day. This will orient the group to the passage being studied.

7. The personal reflection questions are designed to help group members focus on some aspect of their experience. Hopefully, they will help group members to be more aware of the frame of reference and life experience which they bring to the study. The personal reflection section can be done prior to the group meeting or as the first part of the meeting. If the group does not prepare in advance, approximately ten minutes will be needed for individuals to consider these questions.

The personal reflection questions are not designed to be used directly for group discussion. Rather, the first question in the Bible study section is intended to give group members an opportunity to reveal what they feel safe sharing from their time of personal reflection.

8. Read the passage aloud. You may choose to do this yourself, or prior to the study you might ask someone else to read.

9. As you begin to ask the questions in the guide, keep several things in mind. First, the questions are designed to be used just as they are written. If you wish, you may simply read them aloud to the group. Or you may prefer to express them in your own words. However, unnecessary rewording of the questions is not recommended.

Second, the questions are intended to guide the group toward understanding and applying the main idea of the study. You will find the purpose of each study described in the leader's notes. You should try to understand how the study questions and the biblical text work together to lead the group in that direction.

There may be times when it is appropriate to deviate from the study guide. For example, a question may have already been answered. If so, move on to the next question. Or someone may raise an important question not covered in the guide. Take time to discuss it! The important thing is to use discretion. There may be many routes you can travel to reach the goal of the study. But the easiest route is usually the one we have suggested.

10. Don't be afraid of silence. People need time to think about the question before formulating their answers.

11. Draw out a variety of responses from the group. Ask, "Who else has some thoughts about this?" or "How did some of the rest of your respond?" until several people have given answers to the question.

12. Acknowledge all contributions. Try to be affirming whenever possible. Never reject an answer. If it seems clearly wrong to you, ask, "Which part of the text led you to that conclusion?" or "What do the rest of you think?"

13. Realize that not every answer will be addressed to you, even though this will probably happen at first. As group members become more at ease, they will begin to interact more effectively with each other. This is a sign of a healthy discussion.

14. Don't be afraid of controversy. It can be very stimulating. Differences can enrich our lives. If you don't resolve an issue completely, don't be frustrated. Move on and keep it in mind for later. A subsequent study may resolve the problem. Or, the issue may not be resolved—not all questions have answers!

15. Stick to the passage under consideration. It should be the source for answering the questions. Discourage the group from unnecessary cross-referencing. Likewise, stick to the subject and avoid going off on tangents.

16. Periodically summarize what the group has said about the topic. This helps to draw together the various ideas mentioned and gives continuity to the study. But be careful not to use summary statements as an opportunity to give a sermon!

17. During the discussion, feel free to share your own responses. Your honesty about your own recovery can set a tone for the group to feel safe in sharing. Be careful not to dominate the time, but do allow time for your own needs as a group member.

18. Each study ends with a time for prayer. There are several ways to handle this time in a group. The person who leads each study could lead the group in a prayer or you could allow time for group participation. Remember that some members of your group may feel uncomfortable about participating in public prayer. It might be helpful to discuss this with the group during your first meeting and to reach some agreement about how to proceed.

19. Realize that trust in a group grows over time. During the first couple meetings, people will be assessing how safe they will feel in the group. Do not be discouraged if people share only superficially at first. The level of trust will grow slowly but steadily.

Listening to Emotional Pain

Life Recovery Guides are designed to take seriously the pain and struggle that is part of life. People will experience a variety of emotions during these studies. Your role as group leader is not to act as a professional counselor. Instead it is to be a friend who listens to emotional pain. Listening is a gift you can give to hurting people. For many, it is not an easy gift to give. The following suggestions can help you listen more effectively to people in emotional pain.

1. Remember that you are not responsible to take the pain away. People in helping relationships often feel that they are being asked to make the other person feel better. This is usually related to the helper's own patterns of not being comfortable with painful feelings.

2. Not only are you not responsible to take the pain away, one of the things people need most is an opportunity to face and to experience the pain in their lives. They have usually spent years denying their pain and running from it. Healing can come when we are able to face our pain in the presence of someone who cares about us. Rather than trying to take the pain away, commit yourself to listening attentively as it is expressed.

3. Realize that some group members may not feel comfortable with expressions of sadness or anger. You may want to acknowledge that such emotions are uncomfortable, but remind the group that part of recovery is to learn to feel and to allow others to feel.

4. Be very cautious about giving answers and advice. Advice and answers may make you feel better or feel competent, but they may also minimize peoples' problems and their painful feelings. Simple solutions rarely work, and they can easily communicate "You should be better now" or "You shouldn't really be talking about this."

5. Be sure to communicate direct affirmation any time people talk about their painful emotions. It takes courage to talk about our pain because it creates anxiety for us. It is a great gift to be trusted by those who are struggling.

The following notes refer to the questions in the Bible study portion of each study:

Study 1. The Experience of Shame. Psalm 31:1-2, 6-16.
Purpose: To understand through the experience of the author the sources of shame and its emotional impact.

Question 2. Shame can result from a wide variety of experiences. In the studies which follow we will focus on the experiences of being exposed ("I am the utter contempt of my neighbors"), the experience of being devalued ("I am forgotten as though I were dead"), and the experience of rejection ("Those who see me on the street flee from me"). The writer also lists being slandered and being conspired against as shame-sources.

Question 3. The results of shame can be quite varied and complex. As the text illustrates, shame usually is experienced in combination with a variety of other emotions, including fear, hopelessness, anger, sadness and powerlessness. The author graphically describes how his experience of shame led to sorrow and anguish which then led to physical weakness. You might ask your group to list other results of shame which they have experienced or observed.

Question 4. Brokenness is a common way of talking about the consequences of shame. It is a kind of damage deep within a person. The broken pottery metaphor emphasizes both the feelings of worthlessness that shame brings (a broken pot is of no value), as well as the feelings of hopelessness associated with shame (a broken pot can't be mended).

Question 6. The author asks for deliverance and for mercy. He asks God to come quickly, to be a "strong fortress," and to guide him. He asks to be saved by God's "unfailing love."

Question 7. The writer thanks God for "seeing my affliction" and for understanding "the anguish of my soul." The author experienced God's attentiveness, understanding and care as helpful in the process of recovery from shame.

Notice that God's role was not necessarily to eliminate the anguish. The author thanks God for "knowing" his anguish, not for making it all go away. He thanks God for not "handing him over to his enemies" and for giving him a "spacious place." When you want to hide, you look for a small space to crawl into. The author experienced, in contrast, a sense of spatial expansiveness. God provided a spacious place for him where he felt safe.

Question 8. Many people respond to shame by wanting to hide. The need for safety, security and protection is preeminent. The author emphasizes, therefore, that God is a fortress and rock of refuge. God is not the one who shames us, but the One who provides protection and refuge for us in times of shame. Don't be surprised if members of your group have learned that God is someone to run from, not to. It may take a time of healing to begin to see that God is on their side. Being able to see God as the author sees him would provide a "safe place" in times of shame.

Study 2. The Shame of Public Exposure. Luke 19:1-9.

Purpose: To experience through the story of Zacchaeus how belonging to God's family can contribute to recovery from shame.

Question 2. Zacchaeus was a wealthy chief tax collector. Taxes paid by the Jewish population went to the Roman army which occupied the area. To become wealthy as a tax collector Zacchaeus had to collect money from his fellow Jews in excess of what the Romans demanded from him. He was able to make a lot of money that way because he could always threaten reluctant citizens by calling in the Roman military authorities. Thus, he was hated by most of the community as a collaborator with the enemy.

Question 3. The average person in Jesus' day shared the Pharisees' assumption that religiously scrupulous people were special objects of God's affection and that sinners were special objects of God's wrath. To call Zacchaeus a sinner, therefore, was to publicly expose him as defective, rejected both by God and by the community.

Notice that the crowd "mutters"—a very dysfunctional communication style. This kind of demeaning comment is indirect, behind one's back. The previous study (Psalm 31) described shame as the result of being "the utter contempt of my neighbors" and "hearing the slander of many." No doubt Zacchaeus had a similar experience.

Question 4. Jesus does not reject Zacchaeus. Jesus stops under the tree, looks up at Zacchaeus and invites himself to his home. Jesus chooses to associate with Zacchaeus and in so doing, Jesus makes a dramatic statement about Zacchaeus' value as a person. In this way, Jesus publicly identifies with Zacchaeus and honors him by going to his home. Recovery from shame-inducing public exposure is fostered by Jesus' public response of grace.

Question 5. Jesus' public acceptance has a dramatic effect on Zacchaeus. A common effect of shame is to "bind" a person, making emotions and behaviors constricted or ritualized. Grace "unbinds" us and makes new kinds of relationships possible. In this case, Zacchaeus makes new commitments to economic justice and concern for the poor. These commitments represent the adoption of the values of the kingdom of God. Freedom from the bondage of shame leads to both a revised self-concept and to a restructuring of Zacchaeus' social, political and economic world. Recovery from shame begins with learning new and more fully Christian ways of thinking and feeling about ourselves and leads us to commit our lives more fully to God's kingdom.

Question 6. Experiences of shame commonly lead people to believe that they don't belong. Jesus says explicitly that Zacchaeus belongs. Zacchaeus has an identity that is important. He has much in common with those who are now shaming him. Rather than publicly shaming Zacchaeus, Jesus identifies with him, goes to his home, affirms his identity as a son of Abraham and uses the occasion to proclaim salvation.

Question 7. People driven into hiding by experiences of shame are not abandoned by God. Our faults and deficiencies do not lead God to shame us. God will seek us out. God will act on our behalf in our struggle to recover from shame.

Question 8. Many people who have experienced shame expect that God will also shame them. They mistake the shaming voices in their "crowd" for the voice of God. Rather than grace, they expect judgment. Acknowledge the element of surprise that is part of this story: Jesus identifies with sinners and spends time in their company.

Question 9. Be aware that some people will shame themselves if they

they are unable to respond to this exercise. Many people will find it very difficult to experience this kind of direct love from God even though they are Christians. Acknowledge that it takes a long time for the Good News to sink deep within us. Encourage people to accept themselves wherever they are in the process of recovery from shame.

Study 3. The Shame of Being Devalued. Luke 7:36-50.

Purpose: To experience how God's valuing of us helps us to recover from shame.

Question 2. Simon takes Jesus' behavior to be a sign of Jesus' lack of knowledge about the woman. If he were a prophet, he reasoned, he would know these things. A more fundamental assumption is that people who associate with "bad people" are "bad" themselves. Doubts are raised in his mind as to whether Jesus could be a genuine prophet if he did not understand what Simon believed to be a fundamental tenet of religion.

Question 3. Simon's concrete thinking is evident. The woman is a sinner, and therefore has little value. Although the text says that Simon spoke "to himself," nonverbal and indirect communication can still be very effective. Both Jesus and the woman knew the public stance of the Pharisees about the nature of righteousness, so Simon did not need to say much to shame her.

Question 4. The story is about love and forgiveness. Simon was not focused on love and forgiveness but on evaluations and judgments based on moral purity. Jesus is not inattentive to righteousness, but he shapes his concerns very differently. On the prohibition of judgmentalism see Matthew 7:1-5 and James 4:11-12.

Question 5. Jesus' point is not about physical vision. Rather Simon's values and commitments made certain people effectively "invisible" to him. They did not count. They had no value. They were "sinners."

Question 6. Jesus spoke to her, valued her, forgave her. Unlike Simon, Jesus *saw* the woman. He saw her as a person created by God, loved, valued, capable of loving in return. He accepted her love. Jesus did not evaluate her or judge her in ways that produce shame. And he was moved by her love.

Study 4. The Shame of Rejection. Acts 11:1-18.

Purpose: To experience how God's acceptance can contribute to our recovery from shame.

Question 2. Rejection makes a person feel like an outsider. Outsiders are viewed as not good enough to belong. No matter how hard they try, they can't get it right. No doubt Cornelius had wondered if God also rejected him. Rejection results not only in sadness, anger, confusion and self-doubt, but often leads to perfectionism. The assumption of perfectionists is that if only I can get it perfect, if only I can do enough, if only. . . . , then I will be accepted. Encourage people to talk about their own experiences of rejection.

Question 3. The early church apparently accepted circumcised converts to Judaism (see, for example, Acts 6:5) but did not understand God's intentions to include non-Jews into his family. To be excluded is always a painful experience. But, when rejection comes from an authority figure (a parent, a teacher, a boss), it is particularly painful. When the exclusion is justified by appeal to divine authority, the consequences can be even more significant. The message is, "Not only do I reject you, the community of the faithful rejects you, and God rejects you as well." If this is true, then all hope is gone.

Question 4. God went out of his way to make it very clear that he accepted Cornelius and his household. He gave Peter a remarkable vision, arranged a meeting with Cornelius and dramatically demonstrated the presence of the Holy Spirit. This was not the first time God had intervened to make it clear that his love and acceptance extended beyond the house of Abraham. From the very beginning God made it clear that he chose Abraham in order that "all peoples on earth will be blessed" (Gen 12:3). The prophets repeatedly reminded God's people that their missionary calling was rooted in

God's love for all peoples (see, for example, Amos 9:7; Jonah 4:11; Isaiah 49:6).

Question 5. It may be difficult to appreciate the meaning for Peter of his visit to and meal with a non-Jew. He violated a widely accepted social norm and gave a dramatic demonstration of acceptance. The impact on Cornelius would have been a profound mixture of relief, disbelief, joy, hope and amazement.

Question 6. Rejection is a social experience. The formal recognition of Cornelius' standing in God's family was essential to his full recovery. It might be helpful to explore the reality that recovery is a social process. It can't be done in private.

Question 7. God's acceptance may stand in sharp contrast to what people have experienced from family, from peers and even from the church. It is very good news, but it may take a long time to sink deep within us. Experiencing God's acceptance of us is a life-long journey to freedom and joy. The goal for today's study is not to finish the journey but to take the next step!

Study 5. Internalized Shame. Luke 15:11-24.

Purpose: To experience, through the parable of the waiting father, how God's compassion can contribute to our recovery from shame.

Question 2. The son's speech is suggestive of repentance. He says, "I have sinned." He has moved out of denying his situation, sees his desperate state and is looking for help. However, the son's speech also includes elements of internalized shame. The son concludes that he is "not worthy" and that he can no longer be a part of his family.

Question 3. Internalized shame does not always manifest itself as low self-esteem or a sense of unworthiness. People may also express internalized shame in perfectionism, in blaming or in depression. Help people in your group to think about their own tendencies to shame themselves. How do they react to their own brokenness?

Question 4. The son hopes that his father will provide work and food for him. But he expects rejection as a member of the family. He expects a difficult meeting full of shame. He does not expect the extravagant welcome he receives.

Question 5. Encourage the group to list each action of the father and to discuss its significance to the son. Notice that the father's actions precede the shame-filled speech the son intended to make.

> The boy begins to repeat the words of his pre-determined confession. But before he can complete what he intends to say, his father interrupts him. . . . The father expresses the reason for his joy in what seems to be extravagant language. His son was dead but has come to life, he was lost, but has been found . . . the language certainly suggests that the son had announced his intention never to return and that therefore he was as good as dead. His unexpected return leads to great rejoicing. (I. H. Marshall, *The Gospel of Luke* [Grand Rapids, Mich.: Eerdmans, 1979], pp. 610-611.)

Question 6. The contrast between the son's self-rejection and the father's overwhelming acceptance and honoring of the son is the central drama of this story.

Question 7. People who have internalized shame will find it very difficult to comprehend that God loves, rather than hates, them and that God rejoices over, rather than rejects, them. This is a truth we need to come back to over and over again in order to let it slowly change how we see ourselves and how we see God.

Question 8. The focus of this story is on the father's compassion and love. When we sin, we can focus on our failings and heap shame on ourselves, or we can focus on God's compassion and love for us. The Enemy of faith, the Accuser, would have us shame ourselves without mercy and thus never fully experience the joy and freedom offered us by God. Gradually learning to focus more and more on God's love in our times of need and guilt is one thing we can do to make progress in our journey out of shame.

Study 6. God's Love for Those in Shame. Romans 8:31-39.
Purpose: To experience how God's love can contribute to our re-

covery from shame.

Question 3. The sources of condemnation in our lives may be quite varied—parents, employers, teachers, colleagues, friends, lovers, competitors. You may want to remind group members of the ways condemnation has figured in the three previous studies: the crowd was ready to condemn Zacchaeus, the woman who washed Jesus' feet was condemned by the Pharisees, and the prodigal had internalized the condemnation he expected from his father. Encourage the members of your group to identify sources of condemnation in their lives and to explore how these sources have affected them.

Question 4. The text makes it clear that God does not reject or shame us when we experience difficult times in life. Encourage the group to think of specific times of trouble and hardship they have experienced.

Question 6. Fundamentally, we can experience security because we cannot be separated from God's love for us. Paul gives three specific reasons for this assurance. First, having given us his Son, God will surely not withhold other gracious gifts. Second, our accusers have no power over us because God has already entered a verdict of "not guilty." Third, we have a powerful intercessor at the "right hand of God" who is "for us." Encourage the group to reflect on the significance of these sources of security.

Question 7. The word *conquerors* is almost certain to trigger shame in people who have a long history of shame. The logic goes like this: "I should feel like a conqueror. Good Christians should be happy all the time. I should be experiencing every day with Jesus as sweeter than the day before. Since I do not experience that, something must be wrong with me." But that is not at all what the text is saying. The point here is that Christ's victory has made it possible for us to have a security in God's love that can weather the storms of life. We will still feel the storms. We will sometimes "face death all day long," but even in the midst of death we can rest securely in the arms of the One who has faced death and conquered it by God's power.

For more information about Christian resources for people in recovery and subscription information for STEPS, *the newsletter of the National Association for Christian Recovery, we invite you to write to:*

The National Association for Christian Recovery
P.O. Box 11095
Whittier, California 90603

LIFE RECOVERY GUIDES FROM INTER-VARSITY PRESS
By Dale and Juanita Ryan

Recovery from Abuse. Does the nightmare of abuse ever end? After emotional, verbal and/or physical abuse how can you develop secure relationships? Recovery is difficult but possible. This guide will help you turn to God as you put the broken pieces of your life back together again. Six studies, 64 pages, 1158-3.

Recovery from Addictions. Addictions have always been part of the human predicament. Chemicals, food, people, sex, work, spending, gambling, religious practices and more can enslave us. This guide will help you find the wholeness and restoration that God offers to those who are struggling with addictions. Six studies, 64 pages, 1155-9.

Recovery from Bitterness. Sometimes forgiveness gets blocked, stuck, restrained and entangled. We find our hearts turning toward bitterness and revenge. Our inability to forgive can make us feel like spiritual failures. This guide will help us find the strength to change bitterness into forgiveness. Six studies, 64 pages, 1154-0.

Recovery from Codependency. The fear, anger and helplessness people feel when someone they love is addicted can lead to desperate attempts to take care of, or control, the loved one. Both the addicted person's behavior and the frenzied codependent behavior progress in a destructive downward spiral of denial and blame. This guide will help you to let go of over-responsibility and entrust the people you love to God. Six studies, 64 pages, 1156-7.

Recovery from Distorted Images of God. In a world of sin and hate it is difficult for us to understand who the God of love is. These distortions interfere with our ability to express our feelings to God and to trust him. This guide helps us to identify the distortions we have and to come to a new understanding of who God is. Six studies, 64 pages, 1152-4.

Recovery from Family Dysfunctions. Dysfunctional patterns of relating learned early in life affect all of our relationships. We trust God and others less than we wish. This guide offers healing from the pain of the past and acceptance into God's family. Six studies, 64 pages, 1151-6.

Recovery from Loss. Disappointment, unmet expectations, physical or emotional illness and death are all examples of losses that occur in our lives. Working through grief does not help us to forget what we have lost, but it does help us grow in understanding, compassion and courage in the midst of loss. This guide will show you how to receive the comfort God offers. Six studies, 64 pages, 1157-5.

Recovery from Shame. Shame is a social experience. Whatever its source, shame causes people to see themselves as unloveable, unworthy and irreparable. This guide will help you to reform your self-understanding in the light of God's unconditional acceptance. Six studies, 64 pages, 1153-2.